WRITERS REPUBLIC

LEARNING LIFE

40th Anniversary Edition

POETRY BY BRIAN RAYMENT

Copyright © 2021 by Brian Rayment.

All rights reserved. No part of this book may be reproduced in any form or by any electronic or mechanical means, including information storage and retrieval systems, without permission in writing from the publisher, except by reviewers, who may quote brief passages in a review.

This publication contains the opinions and ideas of its author. It is intended to provide helpful and informative material on the subjects addressed in the publication. The author and publisher specifically disclaim all responsibility for any liability, loss, or risk, personal or otherwise, which is incurred as a consequence, directly or indirectly, of the use and application of any of the contents of this book.

Writers Republic L.L.C.
515 Summit Ave. Unit R1
Union City, NJ 07087, USA
Website: www.writersrepublic.com
Hotline: 1-877-656-6838
Email: info@writersrepublic.com

Ordering Information:
Quantity sales. Special discounts are available on quantity purchases by corporations, associations, and others. For details, contact the publisher at the address above.

Library of Congress Control Number: 2021935899
ISBN-13:   978-1-63728-057-7   [Paperback Edition]
   978-1-63728-058-4   [Digital Edition]

Rev. date: 04/28/2021

This is for
George and Joan
Now past
But still my home
For how would I know
Of being alone
Without George and Joan

Table of Contents

Part One
Sowing Seeds

Family	3
Dreamers	5
I Never Thought	6
Purpose	7
Sowing Seeds	8
Why me	10
Wanting	11
Labels	12
Persevere	14
Acceptance	15
Only	16
Let It Go	17
Doubt	18
Light Of Day	19
Human Weakness and the New Generation	20
Use Me	21
Riddles	22
It Hurts	23
Writing	24

Part Two
Grow

Shadow	27
Learning Life	28
My Love	30
Not Me	31
Love Me Please	32
Flower	33
Sprouting	34
Snowflake	35
Nature	36

Sweet Treason	37
Who	38
Poetry	39
No Choice	40
We All	41
Gifts	42
Attitude	43
Dream Waking	44
Trying	45
A New World	46
Going With The Flow	47
Dreaming	48
Looking Into Eve	49
Giving in	50
Mental Wellness	51
Free Ourselves	52
Bringing love home	53

Part One

Sowing Seeds

Family

It is nice to have a family
As caring and loving as mine
Brothers and sisters getting along
Mom and dad are fine

They have given to me
The love I have had
To make good of my time

To give my love
As they are giving
To make our life
The more worth living

Dreamers

There are many dreamers in life I trust
In dreams and how we see
That we all have dreams and lust
The need to live and be
If I could inspire or reach to one
Who sees the way I want to come
If I could change myself so then
It could relate to other men
My character would build and show
Perhaps in dreaming we may grow
If then I find this dream is real
I would give, in thought reveal
The pleasure in the changing
The measure and the ranging
Of heights to reach and thoughts to teach
Knowing of the love in each
Power to enjoy the way
In which we see so far
And fulfilment we receive the day
We dream the way we are

I Never Thought

I never thought it could be this way
My thoughts were getting carried away
And wish to tell you how good it feels
To find my thoughts are very real

I used to think not too much
Seems my feelings were not in touch
It was very confusing feelings refusing
My thoughts were unreal my feelings would feel

As my thoughts became stronger
My feelings would ponder
What could I reveal
If my thoughts are real

Feelings backed off thoughts didn't carry
And now it seems not quite so scary
Quite a process we may go through
Before we find our thoughts are true

Purpose

If you are looking for love
You need only look inside
It is not in the sky above
It is in the heart it hides

If you are looking for reason
You need only react
You know it will be pleasing
Not putting on an act

If you are looking for purpose
It is all in you
Underneath the surface
Purpose will come true

It is true you will find
When with love you start
And with reason in your mind
The purpose in your heart

Sowing Seeds

Sowing seeds is fine and we have to fertilize
Pulling weeds takes time before the seeds arrive
For if we plant where weeds still grow
Seeds will die or grow too slow

We have stunted growth and mutations
In our fields of our nations
Lets plow the fields lets turn the soil
Lets have our harvest yield and have it not spoil

It is hard to build good earth
But beauty is always worth
The work and strain to clear the land
When we know it is for man

For good and proper life to be
We need to set our senses free
Explore our nature and stars above
Explore the deepest depths of love

And in the passage to the end
We make the plants and weeds our friends
We find no false or withered leaf
We find only those without belief

If we believe that they are true
We may be able to help them through
If we have faith and believe in them
It makes their beginning our just end

Then we sow seeds ripened for grow
We sow seeds and weeds both
We look for mix and inner breeding
Our whole crop will be succeeding

Why me

People ask
When they are not treated fair
The world is together
Why cant we share

All the why mes
Can come together
Through openness and understanding
It becomes better

Through tolerance and acceptance
It gets easier to see
Everyone is asking
Why me

Wanting

Wanting so much to give
But all that I have is yours
And everyone else who lives
Belong and deserve so much more

Not meaning to disrupt or disturb
I simply would like to be heard
Not meaning to hurt or display
I simply have something to say

So please if you will respect
We may find we have more than the net
But the sum of whats here and whats next
Without knowing of what to expect

Labels

In my lifetime I have met labels
Though now fables
So just to remind you of what is not right
I will go over a few looking back in my sight

Christine had worn braces on her teeth while in school
Kids would make faces who were the fools
Diane had one arm she wore a hook on the other
I only imagine the hurt she may cover

Steve was a bit odd nothing major mind you
Others found it hard so Steve got it too
Kids in the group home just up the street
In the schoolyard would roam cause others thought them creeps

Lennie is a freak from taking so many drugs
Hangs out on the street with the other thugs
When they are with him good times they spend
Behind his back they tease him and he thinks they are friends

Julie is an epileptic her mother disowns her
No wonder she gets it her mom never phones her
People do not treat her like an ordinary person
If only they meet her she may well stop her cursing

Van is a drinker but he is intact
Some think he is a stinker living like that

Why
Do people make labels and judgements this way
How is this to enable anyone to feel okay
Sure they have problems but do we not all
How would you like to labeled how would you like to fall

This makes me so angry
And want to shout out
It is not in the labels
It is the others I doubt

Persevere

What is it you know
That makes you persevere
On through the day
On through the year

Living as one
With no one else knowing
Refusing to run
Fighting my growing

Acceptance

An alcoholic pothead poet nurse
It could be better it could be worse
Sometimes I think my life is a curse
Living on my dream to verse

I am many things to many people
I have my weakness and my good parts
I am no loser a no good boozer
But booze can console my heart

It brings me down and settles me
With my thoughts and dreams
It keeps me to myself
And shows me loud and screams

Then without my drink of choice
I wallow in the fear
Of not being accepted
As I am right now right here

Only

Only if I did not rely
So much on how it is I try
Only if I did not have responsibility
Would my soul deny me

Only if I did not think
Only if my own instinct
Did not work or was not there
Would I believe I do not care

Only if I try to shove
Only if I debate my love
Only if I try to smoother
Would my heart I cover

Only if I did not act
On my values and my motives
Only if I withhold the facts
Would I have no reason to give

Let It Go

I have it in my hand
I have it in my heart
I have it in my thoughts
I had it from the start

Let it go
And be beside love
Let it go
You cant decide love

If this is what is meant to be
Let love go inside of me
Let love grow unselfishly
Let love know its destiny

If love is common to us all
How can I profess it
If love is wise and love is all
How can I possess it

Doubt

I don't know why I am so afraid
Of sharing thoughts with you
You seem so strong and self directed
So honest and so true

I often think that if I show
My weakness and my doubt
That if you let me in your heart
You then would kick me out

Light Of Day

I do not mean to frighten you
Or direct the way you choose
I only wish to share with you
The way the heavens soothe

Paths are different but minds are one
When we know what is right
When light grows and lightens so
It makes the light so bright

We never doubt the power of God
Or power he chooses to flow
And often he does have the right
For touchstones in the glow

It is not for you or I to use
In any other way
But for paradox and shinning
In the light of day

Of course it fades
As days pass by in time
But stays to shade let others in
If only through a rhyme

Human Weakness and the New Generation

Hippies in the sixties rock and roll music
Individuality seems to fit
The difference love flower power
Seeing a new way a new morality

Drugs and rebellion was how we relate
To our elders about what we hate
Going by the rules listening to the fools
Living in the past making it last

Times have changed we have grown
Let us learn from what we have shown
We are capable to run our lives
We know what we need to survive

Lets show some power in us that is true
By what we know and what we do
Open our minds to the many others we see
And the way they are free

Lets make it a ritual
To learn more than past generations
Slack off on condemnations
Respect everyone gain understanding
By being ourselves and demanding more

Use Me

Use me
To find yourself
It is no problem
It is no help

I am a tool
To better mankind
This is my life
Do not think I am kind

Riddles

Love is deep from pain it weeps
When we cry we find it keeps
Our faith to see a warm soft rain
And how it helps our love maintain

Hate is true in all of us
We all do hate why the fuss
Aggression is natural a driving force
In learning to control it we find its source

Relationships are all alike
We help each other so we might
Show each other what we already know
Becoming free we come to show

Dreams are real if they are true
Scenes in a reel a movie that is you
Vision is real it came from whence
We look what we give and what we have spent

It Hurts

I love so much it hurts
With no one else to share
My heart fills up with sorrow
When no one seems to care

I love so much to give
I love to give away
My actions and myself
As I am from day to day

I have so many good things
In me to pass along
I have so many voices
My life becomes a song

Writing

I wrote a journal for many years
Past memories and fears
Pains of growing and accepting things
Pains of being the way I was being

and it just goes to show
how far one can go
when they decide
its time to grow

exploring thoughts of love in time
feeling till we feel a sign
that there is something more to you
that there is something else that moves

you find there is more to you than you
and then what are you to do

Part Two

Grow

Shadow

Shadow sits outside the door
Straight and looking out
Barking at the kids across the street
Hoping they will come to meet
Her and play around
Shadow likes the kids in town

Shadow has one ear up
And one ear down
Shadow has yet
To learn to get down
When she jumps up

Shadow chews and bites
Shadow licks and likes
It when I give her treats
Shadow is sweet

She sleeps and plays all day long
Pulls me around thinking she is strong
Drags her tail when I say she is wrong
Shadow is my pup

Learning Life

As we grow to find what we do
We look for answers to find what is true
Happiness love peace of mind
Is learning but a different kind

Giving and sharing our thoughts
Living and caring never stops
We meet friends and count on them
We find dependence with other men

Taking care of our lives learning how to survive
Is life in a very true sense
Books and minds are part of whence
We are coming from we are learning some
We go no further if we think we are done

Searching deeper to find beliefs
In ourselves is how we teach
Ourselves and others learning life
Through the good and through the strife

We learn trust we are honest
We learn how to be our best
We learn tolerance we can accept
Others if they are not with us yet

We give and receive
we do not play games
What we perceive is what remains

There are stages of growth in mind and body
Stages of consciousness and we are the lobby
To blend together many parts
To live from our mind and from our heart

To live and learn to ask advice
To really know we all learn life

My Love

My love is me and what I see
My love is life and setting it free
My love is yours if you want it
My love is not for me to flaunt it

My love is truth to me that is
My love is action in how I live
My love can hurt I am very critical
My love may help to find your will

My love is mine I have so much
My love is received from others touch
My love is sharing what I know
My love is caring for how we grow

My love is deep and with God
My love to feel is very hard
My love connects with me at birth
My love is rooted to our earth

My love is for me and everyone else
My love is risking the love in yourself
My love is one and with the land
My love is one that shows my hand

Not Me

Who paints the scenery in the sky
Or causes thunder clouds to cry
Who feeds the trees that grow so high
Who makes a worm a butterfly

Who straightens out a mad young punk
Who sobers up a useless drunk
Who slows the speed in an addicts life
Who frees the tortured battered wife

Not me who heals the sick and dying
All I can do is keep on trying
Not me who finds the winning ticket
I only look and try to pick it

Who lets me be so real and true
Then gives me troubles to go through
Who follows me and picks me up
When I fall down on luck

Not me has the strength of love
Not me paints the sky above
Not me frees the mind and soul
Although I do share this goal

Love Me Please

Trying to be myself
Learning day to day
Praying what I am is good
Risking I know the way

Wanting to go on like this
Needing to be free
Hoping you can share my thoughts
On a time in me

When now for love is on my mind
When ink is my medium
Between toil and work
Between this world of mine

Take away my troubles please
Now for love me on this eve
Understand the yearning
See the fire burning

Flower

If I say
I love you so
Would you believe it is true

If I send another poem
Would you feel so not alone

If I keep writing
Would you stop fighting
Would you open your bud
Would you not turn sour

If I keep talking
Would you listen
Just for my sake
Just for my self

If I keep growing
If I keep showing
If I keep feeding
Would you flower

Sprouting

I can change me
You watch and see
The way I am will grow more
I can change me
I can show me
I can show you
What I am about
I can do it no doubt
I can show me
I can give me
I can give what I feel
I can give that I am real
I can give me
I can share me
I can give me to you
I can love you
I do
I can share me
I can care about me
I can do what I need
I can really succeed
I can care about me
I can grow me
I can sprout a good seed
I can give what you need
I can grow me

Snowflake

Like many ways a snowflake forms
An image of ourself is born
God shows in many different ways
He gives in each of us to pray

To thank him for this life received
To trust in him the truth he sees

Many seconds in our time
Can fill our hearts with love in mind
Can let us breathe the warm sunshine
Then let it flow into a rhyme

Nature

It happens every moment
I look out at a tree
I say how can you do it
It says right back to me

Whatever you wish can form a branch
Truth will hold the roots
Every shiver every glance
Enhances all the fruit

Create yourself what I endure
Feed on the thought of earth
Feel the flowing overture
When nature shows its worth

Sweet Treason

Poetry is a wonderous tool practicing the golden rule
Bringing beauty and thoughts intense
Bringing thou art from thou art whence
So that we may endure seeping in our life so pure
So that we may reflect on power of the intellect

The strength and lust for fortitude
The peace and present solitude
The pleasure of lifes interlude
In which the senses have been brewed

To mix and flow to grow and blend
To start anew including the end
To startle and shake to arouse and interest
To become involved in life continuous

Riches how a verse endowed
Makes life speaks so very loud
Or contrast of the soft reminder
Of what is making this verse kinder

Love that weeps and fights its way
Can find no more or better prey
Than that of peace and that of rhyme
In which the fight will dwindle into time

Who

Who can I relate to
Who can hear and see
Who can love me back
Who can let me be

Who can I share with
Who can grow in love
Who can I care with
Who can feel the call

Who can I confess to
Who can I give in to
Who can I rest with
Who can I show

Poetry

If I could come right out and say
My life needs to be this way
If I could show I mean no harm
If I could create no alarm
How would I wake up

If I could come right out and say
My life needs to be this way
If I could show I am alright
If I could show how true I am
How would I be human

If I could show im insecure
If I could show im weak but pure
If I could show I need and need
If I could grow yet still a seed
How I would be pleased

No Choice

I cannot pick who I love
I cannot change the weather
I can not choose the songs for birds
Or change their color of feather

There is no choice in this life
Our minds are made already
Our hearts and bodies know the answers
Our love is strong and steady

We cannot choose the direction a river may flow
Or pick our path where no road goes
But as we see obstructions gone
We find our love where it belongs

For all things the way they are
Reflect in changes growing
Turning scars into stars
Receiving light still glowing

We cannot pick who we love
We cannot change the weather
We cannot choose the songs for birds
Or change their color of feather

We All

We all like to give
And share what we know
And powerful examples
Help us to show

The unselfish deeds
And thoughts that bear fruit
Fulfilling Gods need
Right at the root

Feelings of love
Overflow any questions
Showing by action
Teaching the lessons

What you give to me today
I will love and give away
The growth that I receive
On the morning of this eve

Gifts

I received a gift one day it means so much to me
A child gave to me a picture it was of a tree
One day while helping someone out I got this terrific rush
Up my spine from my toes I could not help but blush

Once someone gave to me permission
To talk and act my way
No longer do I feel submission
With the gift received that day

If I could think of all the gifts
I have been given up to now
It makes my eyes glow with bliss
Knowing this is how

We receive reward for giving ourselves
We gain wealth in how we live
We remember feeling and true gain
By what others give

Attitude

I Care, is such a simple attitude
Yet can be hard to understand
How we care is not the same
For each and every man

Words are often spoken
But without thought at first
That is why sometimes people swear
And sometimes they subvert

When I hear another say
"I don't really care"
I tend to believe in every way
Something is not fair

Often we have fickle moods
And slumber through our day
As humans we are not perfect
In sometimes what we say

But if we always keep in mind
It is our life we share
Surely we will find the time
To speak, because we Care

Dream Waking

I spend the day dream waking
Practising the steps in taking
Actions to begin the day

Dreaming through the day I find
I live not only through the mind
I live in heart action doing
I live each day renewing

Realities of higher sources
Flavoring this life
Living on todays resources
Breathing in is nice

I take in what I need to live
I give what I have to share
My dream awakens as I love
I care I care I care

When I peak I go to sleep
And rest as natures whole
Comforts me and gives soul rest
I dream awake, I know

Trying

My mind goes on and on
Into eternity
My soul is searching for a song
To bring tranquility

My feelings flow with love so deep
It frightens me sometimes
I get to feeling out of myself
And into others kind

Sometimes I tire and fade away
Almost ready to give up
Nothing left but today
This moments loving touch

What a way to live my life
Not knowing what is to come
Hoping that I am doing right
Trying not to run

A New World

I went out of a world today
It was hard to leave behind
My focus somehow lost I pray
The true world in my mind

This world is getting stronger now
As I share today
Lasting longer knowing how
These other worlds not that far away

Each day I accept a little more
Of going with the flow
Each day I surrender my own will
Each day I let it go

A new world opens up to me
A new world shows itself
A new world catches hold of me
A world of warmth and wealth

I have as yet to grasp this world
And hold it forever still
I only need not mask this world
And it will show its will

Going With The Flow

I am going with the flow
Of my inner stream
It has come that I know
From where I have been

I still need to learn
How to use the whole me
I still need
To let myself be

I cannot feel this flow
But I know it is here
I still need to grow
To handle this fear

Inner streams have direction
I have as yet to find mine
It may come from reflection
In my own mind

It is still only to me
What it seems
If I can just let it be
I may find what it means

Dreaming

I started to dream along time ago
I was going fast while told to go slow
I was learning things from myself and others
I was believing we all are brothers

It bothered me when things were not fair
It bothered me why some just don't care
I started caring and found it is true
When you really care your dreams will come through

To make more than illusion
To make more than an act
To make peace from confusion
To make now where you are at

I saw heaven on earth
I saw beauty in the beast
I saw what we are worth
I saw more from the least

If others could see it
I would not have to scheme
If others could believe it
I would not have to dream

Looking Into Eve

Stars and night air bring to mind
Unknown worlds beyond the fine
Line of the limit we perceive
into everlasting eve

of miracles and sacred souls
resting into natures whole
feeling peace and no disorder
knowing part of all

Giving in

Now im older things have been changing
Now im wiser my thoughts are arranging
New ways to manage to way to hope
New ways to see things new ways to cope

My will was too strong my motives were selfish
My goals were a song my dream was a wish
Through trial and error I discovered more
My ship would not leave while stranded on shore

I had to give in I had to give up
I had to let wind fill my sails up
It was not easy pride interrupted
But the wind had got breezy and waves had irrupted

My ship had set sail my ego was gone
Myself no avail it was God who was strong
All I need to was to conform to his will
To show I was true and let my heart fill

With his care for me and our care for others
With his goal you see I care for all brothers

The hole in my soul is now filling up
With his goal for me he is tipping my cup
He has forgiven my selfish ways
He has turned learning into praise

Mental Wellness

Mental wellness
It is no wonder
Some of us do go under
And never come up with what they see

They are different they are odd
But knowing they are human is not hard
They have idiosyncrasies that we do not see
In makes some laugh at them and hope
That they go or that they know
They are not the same they are too sane

They need love they need attention
They need very much apprehension
To see similarities between them and i
To really ask the question why

To get together one to one
To maybe have some real live fun
To see they really are okay
Though they may not seem this way

Everyone is human everyone is fine
Be the kind to spend some time
In whatever relationship you are alike
As long as you do not fight to find judgements or labels
To keep true old fables

Free Ourselves

We all need to free ourselves
Give our life a gift
We all need to be ourselves
Give our life a lift

We all need to see ourselves
As something more than tools
We all need to key ourselves
And free our happy fools

We all need to open up
To ways of flying and seeing
We all need to just relax
And be in our own being

We can really build ourselves
With our fools in we
So that we can rule ourselves
To be and just to be

We can really live today
And give and give and give
We can really free ourselves
And live and live and live

Bringing love home

Love to me is like the warmth
You feel in front of a fire
While camping out or cuddled inside
Whatever you may desire

I love to sit down by the lake
On top of a rock that we call ours
I love the peace reflections create
And sometimes lasts for hours

Walking over beaver dams
Looking for the Big Dipper
Watching mom make homemade jam
Though buying it is quicker

Playing with nieces and nephews of mine
Listening to their unique voices
Playing makes me feel so fine
We have so many choices

Just to sit at home alone
Sleep or read talk on the phone
I really like to make a poem
It seems to bring my love home

CPSIA information can be obtained
at www.ICGtesting.com
Printed in the USA
BVHW032324050521
606478BV00001B/21